Machine Learning in Meteorology and Climate Science

Table of Contents

Chapter 1. Introduction

Special Report: Unraveling the Skies - An Intriguing Look into Machine Learning in Meteorology and Climate Science

In this exclusive special report, we peel back the layers of the usually high-tech worlds of meteorology and climate science to reveal their surprising coterie with machine learning. We take an accessible and engaging approach to bring you insights about how the burgeoning field of machine learning is revolutionizing our understanding of weather patterns and climate change. Whether it's refining weather forecasting methodology, providing insightful climate change projections, or improving our disaster response mechanisms, machine learning is surging to the forefront. Without delving too deeply into technical jargon, we offer you a fascinating glimpse into how technology and science have intermingled to provide new pathways in weather prediction and climate studies. By the time you're through this special report, you'll be enthralled by the sky in a whole new light, and you'll appreciate how machine learning is aiding us on this weather-watching journey. Get your copy today and embark on this compelling scientific voyage!

Chapter 2. Introduction to Machine Learning and Climate Science

To understand the synergy between machine learning (ML) and climate science, it's essential first to grasp these individual fields and their importance. Climate science centers around studying earth's weather patterns over protracted periods - from a few years to millions - enabling us to comprehend alterations in the planet's climate system. Machine learning, a subset of artificial intelligence, emphasizes building systems that learn and enhance from experience without explicit programming.

2.1. Climate Science and Its Fundamentals

Earth's climate system is complex. It consists of five primary components: the atmosphere, hydrosphere (water bodies), cryosphere (frozen water regions), biosphere (living organisms), and lithosphere (earth's crust and upper mantle). There's incredible interaction among these elements, engendering a dynamic global climate system. The task of climate science is to comprehend these interactions and changes over time.

Weather, as many would surmise, isn't akin to climate. Whereas weather pertains to short-term atmospheric conditions, climate delineates the 'average weather' in a region over extended periods (decades to millions of years). Thus, the study of climate offers a 'big picture' of temperature patterns, precipitations, wind, and more - allowing us to tackle climate change.

2.2. Machine Learning: A Primer

Machine Learning, typically part of data science, employs statistical techniques to enable computers to improve from experience. This method strives to create a model, from input and output instances, which can subsequently predict outputs given new inputs. In learning, errors are computed, and the model is adjusted to reduce these errors.

Machine learning algorithms are categorized into a few types, depending upon the information available to a learning system:

1. Supervised Learning: Each instance of the input data comes with an associated target value, such as a classification label.

2. Unsupervised Learning: There are no target attributes associated with the input data.

3. Reinforcement Learning: The model learns its behavior based on reward feedback.

The application of machine learning is pervasive, encompassing fields that generations ago would seem unfathomable - meteorology and climate science being two such realms.

2.3. Confluence of Machine Learning and Climate Science

The crux of climate data analysis lies in spotting patterns and trends. Yet, the sheer complexity and volume of climatic data make this analysis a formidable challenge. This is where machine learning strides in, providing robust computational and predictive models that can manage and extract meaningful information from colossal, multilayered data sets.

Researchers and scientists integrate machine learning into climate modeling in two principal capacities. Firstly, machine learning aids in downscaling coarse resolution climate models to localize their findings. Secondly, it helps recognize complex patterns and accelerate climate simulations. By leveraging these capabilities, they can generate high-resolution, precise predictions about future climate conditions.

2.4. Machine Learning in Weather Forecasting

Machine learning holds incredible promise in advancing weather forecasting and understanding. Traditionally, numerical weather prediction models have been the cornerstone of weather forecasts; however, they have certain limitations, such as failing to capture small-scale events and incorporating nowcasting data.

Machine learning algorithms can bridge these chalk-and-cheese differences. They can learn and predict complex non-linear relationships, thereby supplementing and refining traditional weather forecasting methods. For instance, artificial neural networks, a type of machine learning algorithm, are now used to predict daily weather and extreme weather events like hurricanes or cyclones.

2.5. Machine Learning in Climate Change Analysis

Climate change, one of the most pressing issues of our time, poses tremendous challenges, primary among them being the prediction of earth's future climate. Climate models are pivotal here, yet they often overlook many complex physical processes due to computational constraints.

Machine learning algorithms can augment these models, providing a more sophisticated and encompassing predictive power. They can highlight hidden patterns and linkages within climatic variables, facilitating the understanding of climate change better. This enhanced comprehension can lead to more effective mitigation strategies and adaptable climate policies.

In conclusion, the symbiosis between machine learning and climate science promises a hopeful future where our understanding and response to weather patterns and climate change can be honed to a greater extent. Through this prosperous union, we gain the ability to predict, prepare, and possibly even prevent significant negative climate events. As we continue to unravel the intricacies of the sky above, we are guided by the commitment to learn and adapt, like the algorithms we create.

Chapter 3. Behind the Weather: Decoding Predictive Modeling

The past, it is said, is often the best indicator of future conditions, particularly in the field of climatology. Field researchers and meteorologists have long tapped into weather data archives to develop their predictive models. Today's sophisticated technology, however, is only beginning to exploit a novel and powerful tool: machine learning.

Machine learning is no magic wand, but it's opening up intriguing possibilities for meteorology as we understand it today. It's not about replacing traditional models but enhancing them, facilitating the extraction of the most meaningful insights from a vast and complex dataset. To work its magic, machine learning depends on a myriad of algorithms, each leaving its print on the data interpretation.

3.1. Understanding the Basics of Predictive Modeling

Predictive modeling, in simple terms, is about using statistics to predict outcomes. In the realm of meteorology, it includes harnessing atmospheric science, physics, and chemistry to forecast weather patterns. How does Machine Learning feed into it?

Imagine predictive models as complex puzzles. Each piece must fit perfectly to form the final, clear picture. But what if there are missing pieces, or if too many similar-looking pieces confuse you? Here, machine learning thrives. Machine learning algorithms are designed to find patterns in the chaos, filling gaps, and learning from the process, improving their accuracy over time.

3.2. Predictive Modeling's Role in Weather Forecasting

Meteorological data is characterized by high-dimensionality and nonlinearity, making it challenging for traditional statistical methods to provide accurate predictions. However, the ability of machine learning to handle this colossal volume, variety, and veracity of data makes it a clear winner in enhancing predictive modeling methodologies.

From temperature, pressure, and humidity, to wind speed and direction, numerous climate variables contribute to the weather models. Then there are the patterns themselves – series of complex, often nonlinear, interactions that make up the weather. By learning from historical data, machine learning algorithms can discern patterns in weather data, enhancing forecast accuracy. This process provides meteorologists with a more granular understanding of what might lie ahead, strengthening both local and global forecast models.

3.3. Machine Learning Techniques in Predictive Modeling

Various machine learning methods have found their way into meteorological forecasting and climatological studies. Two of the most prevalent ones are supervised and unsupervised learning.

In supervised learning, the output datasets are pre-labeled - the algorithm is guided as it constructs predictive models. On the other hand, unsupervised learning deals with datasets without predefined labels. The algorithm is 'on its own,' finding hidden patterns and structures within the data.

Other techniques include Artificial Neural Networks (ANN), a computational model based on the human brain's neural networks, and Decision Trees, which split complex decisions into multiple binary decisions, effectively creating a decision pathway. The versatility and adaptability of these techniques have made them an integral part of modern-day weather forecasting and climate research.

3.4. Taking Predictive Modeling to the Next Level

The fusion of big data, machine learning, and predictive modeling is unlocking previously unchartered territories in the field of meteorology and climate science. Now, predictions are no longer just a set of numbers. Machine learning algorithms aid researchers in visualizing future scenarios via data simulation, enhancing our understanding of potential climate dynamics.

This convergence has led to the evolution of 'nowcasting' – predicting weather changes over the next few hours – which was previously a major challenge. ML-aided predictive modeling provides high-resolution, region-specific forecasts that boost our readiness to deal with volatile weather conditions, enhance resource management, and even save lives.

Machine learning also intensifies multi-model ensemble forecasts – multiple forecast models run together to give an average prediction, factoring in uncertainties from each model. The machine learning algorithm fine-tunes each individual model, refining the ensemble's performance,

3.5. Conclusion: A Promising Horizon

Applying machine learning to predictive modeling in meteorology is like a master sculptor chipping away at a block of marble. It's a meticulous process of revealing the masterpiece hidden within a coarse, chiseled exterior. Machine learning does not render traditional methods obsolete; it enriches them.

The journey is fraught with challenges. But as the machine learns and evolves, so do our methodologies - they become more sophisticated, accurate, and dynamic. The relentless pursuit for a 'sky truth' via machine learning-trimmed predictive modeling is a captivating, ongoing saga.

As we venture further into this exciting territory, we remain hopeful. With machine learning spun into the meteorology and climate science tapestry, our predictive models will only continue to grow richer, paving the way towards a safer, better-prepared society. And as the algorithms keep learning and growing, we can be assured that the future of weather prediction is dynamic, and incredibly promising. And don't we all want a little bit of certainty about tomorrow's weather?

Chapter 4. Improving Weather Forecasts with Machine Learning

In the field of meteorology, making accurate and reliable weather forecasts is of vital importance. From providing day-to-day weather updates to predicting catastrophic weather events, meteorologists and climatologists rely heavily on a myriad of sophisticated tools. However, the integration of machine learning into the drilling process of weather prediction has ushered in an era of greatly improved forecasting. This chapter delves into the intricate world of machine learning and how its application to meteorology is demonstrably enhancing weather predictions.

4.1. The Birth of Machine Learning in Meteorology

Essentially, machine learning is a subset of artificial intelligence (AI) that provides systems the ability to automatically learn and improve from experience without being explicitly programmed. This feature has made machine learning a natural ally in analyzing the vast amount of data available in the field of meteorology.

In meteorology, predicting even common weather patterns can be a complex process due to the swift and often nonlinear evolution of meteorological conditions. Traditional models struggle with these nonlinearities and with handling the massive volumes of data generated from numerous weather stations, satellites, and atmospheric sensors. Machine learning has filled these gaps, being designed to manage large datasets and perform analysis that can unearth patterns which are usually imperceptible to traditional techniques. As a result, machine learning involvement in meteorology has seen a dramatic rise in improving weather forecasts.

4.2. Machine Learning Techniques in Weather Prediction

As more data volumes and formats come under the fold of meteorological analysis, a variety of machine learning techniques are being used to improve the accuracy of weather predictions. Neural networks, decision trees, and support vector machines are some of these techniques.

Neural networks, for instance, mimic the human brain's ability to learn from experience. They are valuable for analyzing complex, high-dimensional data, offering a notable improvement over standard linear algorithms. Another technique frequently used is decision trees. They establish a tree-like model of decisions, primarily used for rainfall prediction, analyzing weather parameters like relative humidity, air temperature, and wind speed. Support Vector Machines (SVM) segregate data into different classes, providing a useful tool for weather classification tasks.

The implementation of these techniques varies depending on the weather condition in focus, but the overarching aim is the same – to extract meaningful insights from vast meteorological data and provide accurate weather forecasts.

4.3. Improving Accuracy of Weather Forecasts

While machine learning doesn't provide perfect predictions, it substantially improves the accuracy of weather forecasts when compared to traditional techniques. It does this by considering a large number of variables or factors, better replicating the complexity of atmospheric physics.

For example, by applying machine learning models to radar data, we can better predict severe weather events such as thunderstorms, tornadoes, or hail. In addition, machine learning algorithms trained on historical data can provide accurate predictions on seasonal shifts, proving immensely useful in agricultural planning and water resource management.

Moreover, accuracy isn't the only aspect of weather forecasting that benefits from machine learning; it also increases the speed of calculations and analysis. By making sense of huge datasets rapidly, it allows meteorologists to provide real-time forecasts, improving our response time to approaching severe weather scenarios.

4.4. Machine Learning for Long-Term Climate Predictions

Weather forecasting is not just about immediate, short-term predictions. It's also about understanding longer-term climatic patterns. When machine learning is applied to historical weather data and current weather observations, it can help predict long-term climate trends, in turn, assisting in our fight against climate change.

Machine learning algorithms can analyze past climate change events and pollution levels to predict future climate scenarios. These predictive models can assist in understanding and mitigating the effects of global warming, thus providing policy-makers with essential data for informed legislation.

4.5. The Future of Weather Forecasts with Machine Learning

Looking at the current trajectory, it's clear that machine learning will continue to play a pivotal role in advancing meteorology. Machine learning models are evolving. They are being fine-tuned to adapt to new types of data, and they have the potential to greatly influence the accuracy and precision of future weather predictions.

However, like all tools, machine learning also has its limitations. It is dependent on the quality and quantity of the data fed into it. The 'black-box' nature of some algorithms can often make their predictions difficult to interpret and their decision-making process difficult to understand.

Nevertheless, the positives significantly outweigh any limitations. Machine learning, combined with the effort of meteorologists, has already gifted us with some remarkable improvements in weather forecasting. Its future in meteorology certainly seems full of promise; a step towards achieving more reliable, accurate, and quick weather predictions to the benefit of all humanity.

Chapter 5. Climate Change Detection: The Role of Artificial Intelligence

Climate change is one of the most significant and pressing issues of our time, creating an urgent need for reliable and precise prediction models. Over the years, traditional climate models, while effective, have often been unable to consider the vast amounts of data and variations that play decisive roles in affecting climate change. This is where artificial intelligence (AI), primarily machine learning, has begun to influence the field substantially, helping us gain an in-depth understanding of the numerous factors impacting our planet's climate.

5.1. Comprehending Climate Change Through Machine Learning

Machine learning, a subset of AI, excels in recognizing patterns within vast datasets that might be invisible to the human eye or traditional analysis methods. When applied to climate science, it has the potential to significantly enhance our understanding of the various factors contributing to the ever-changing global climate patterns.

Using machine learning to monitor climate change starts with data - oceans of it. Weather observatories, satellites, ocean vessels, and more collect vast amounts of data about the Earth's atmosphere, hydrosphere, and geosphere every day. These humongous datasets are rife with insights about how our planet's climate is changing, and machine learning, with its ability to analyze and find patterns in voluminous datasets, is a powerful tool for climate scientists. Engineers are training algorithms to process this data and provide valuable insights, thereby bringing a new dimension to climate change detection.

Notably, machine learning can handle the non-linearities and complex dynamics that traditional physics-based climate models might find challenging. This ability, paired with its power to process, analyze, and learn from vast amounts of data, makes machine learning an invaluable tool in the climate scientist's arsenal.

5.2. Enhancing Climate Projections

One of the most crucial areas where AI is influencing how we understand climate change is enhancing climate projections. By extrapolating historical climate data into the future, making assumptions about greenhouse gas emissions, and applying complex mathematical models, we aim to estimate future global warming. The limitations of traditional modelling approaches often stem from their linear nature, which doesn't account for the complexity and randomness found in real-world climate systems.

Machine learning's ability to ingest large quantities of data and discern patterns allows it to predict with higher accuracy how human activities and natural phenomena will affect global climate changes. It complements and enhances traditional climate modelling by handling the nonlinear, chaotic systems that propel our climate.

By integrating machine learning with existing climate modelling methods, scientists are developing hybrid systems capable of producing more accurate forecasts. These improved models can predict a broad array of climate variables, from temperature variations to precipitation patterns, thereby fuelling informed policy decisions and disaster management planning.

5.3. Improving Attribution Studies

Climate attribution studies seek to determine how much human activities are responsible for particular events or changes in climate. Until recently, these studies have largely focused on temperature increases. However, the advent of machine learning is opening doors to delve deeper into other critical factors, such as changes in precipitation patterns, severe weather events, and more.

Machine learning possesses the ability to weave through the intricate web of variables and find significant patterns, which can then be used to determine the causes and impacts of these climatic changes with more certainty. By creating detailed, in-depth models, AI allows for highly accurate and comprehensive attribution studies, thus broadening our understanding of how our actions influence the climate on a granular level.

5.4. Informing Policy and Driving Action

Machine learning not only enhances our understanding of climate change but also aids in developing actionable solutions. Accurate predictions can inform policy-making, inspiring ways to mitigate climate change and adapt to its impacts.

For instance, AI can analyze the impacts of different climate policies, quantifying their potential benefits and challenges. This can guide governments and organizations in choosing the most effective strategies for climate change mitigation. Additionally, machine learning's predictive capabilities can help in planning for climate-resistant infrastructure, developing more efficient energy solutions, and improving disaster response mechanisms.

5.5. Conclusion

The implications of machine learning and AI in understanding and confronting climate change are vast and transformative. As we continue to fine-tune these tools, they will undoubtedly play a significant role in shaping how we address this global issue in the years to come. Remember that the fight against climate change is a shared mission, and every improvement in our understanding and prediction of climate phenomena brings us one step closer to a sustainable future for all.

Chapter 6. Understanding Extreme Weather Events with Machine Learning

Our understanding of extreme weather events, their causes and consequences, have immensely improved over the years, thanks to the advances in climate studies. These events, such as hurricanes, floods, and tornados, pose significant threats to lives, infrastructure, and ecosystems. As climate change continues to exacerbate these chronic challenges, accurate, timely prediction of extreme events becomes increasingly critical. This is where machine learning steps in, lending its prowess to meteorologists and climate scientists to help uncover the intricate patterns and predictive indicators of these phenomena.

6.1. Machine Learning and Extreme Weather: An Introduction

Machine learning (ML) has its roots in the field of artificial intelligence (AI). It is an approach where computers are trained to learn from data and subsequently make predictions or decisions without being explicitly programmed to perform such tasks. In recent years, this technology has made remarkable strides in various fields, including weather and climate science. ML is now able to decipher complex atmospheric data, unveiling the unique patterns and factors contributing to extreme weather events.

Utilizing vast meteorological data sets - including atmospheric pressure readings, temperatures, humidity levels, and wind speeds - machine learning algorithms can detect patterns that human analysts may overlook. ML models can be trained to learn from the past events, detect patterns, and predict future occurrences. They are not only instrumental in forecasting inclement weather but also useful in unveiling the intricate ties between disparate weather elements and how these might align to produce extreme conditions.

6.2. Training Machine Learning Models: Unveiling the Patterns

Machine learning's ability to derive insights from big data is at the heart of its potential in weather prediction. Typically, ML systems are trained on an extensive archive of weather data. For more advanced applications like deep learning, the models are designed to learn from the data without being directly input with rules of analysis.

Datasets used can be historical weather data, images from weather satellites, radar readings, and even information gleaned from social media. ML algorithms crunch this enormous amount of data to infer patterns and create predictive models. Over time, and with more data, these models continue to learn and refine their predictions. Machine learning's capability to handle such colossal datasets is incredibly beneficial in predicting extreme weather events, where observations from multiple data sources must be integrated and analyzed in a sophisticated manner.

6.3. Applications: From Prediction to Strategy Development

The benefits of employing machine learning in the realm of meteorology and climate science extend beyond predicting when and where an extreme weather event might occur. By implementing ML models, the forecasts' precision and reliability dramatically increases, which is crucial for strategy development and proactive planning. Accurate predictions can allow for more effective disaster risk reduction efforts, including early warning systems and emergency planning.

An excellent example of this would be the use of ML models in storm tracking. Traditionally, storm tracking has relied heavily on satellite imagery analyzed by meteorologists. With machine learning algorithms in play, a model can be trained to recognize characteristics of storm systems, predict the direction they're likely to move, and suggest possible intensifications in the future. This can significantly improve the lead time and accuracy of severe weather warnings, making communities safer.

Additionally, ML can also assist in modeling the potential damages of extreme weather events, assisting insurance companies, urban planners, and government agencies in their decision-making process. It helps them evaluate the potential risk of extreme events and develop more effective risk management strategies.

6.4. Extreme Weather Events & Climate Change: Connecting the Dots

Machine learning also has an important role to play in climate change studies. ML can help scientists understand the relationships between extreme weather events and long-term changes in the climate. By correlating the frequency and intensity of these events with global warming indicators, machine learning models can produce robust predictions about future climate patterns. This capability is essential for preparedness, mitigation, and adaptation strategies in the face of climate change.

In a nutshell, machine learning, with its advanced algorithms and vast data processing capabilities, is augmenting our ability to predict and manage extreme weather events. As advancements continue and more data becomes available, predictions are bound to become more accurate, timely, and crucial than ever before in our quest to safeguard our planet and its inhabitants. Thanks to ML, we are now equipped with better tools to unravel the secrets held by our skies.

Chapter 7. Using Machine Learning to Monitor Environmental Changes

Defining our current age as the 'Anthropocene' – a geological era articulated by human activity, gives due credit to the monumental impact humanity has had on the global climate. The variegated effects of this human imposition have compelled scientists and researchers to scrutinize the domains of meteorology and climatology in greater detail.

7.1. Utilising Machine Learning To Detect Changes

Machine learning (ML) techniques are an increasingly popular instrument in this process. Relying on large and diverse datasets, they can identify trends and patterns beyond human scale or comprehension. Unsurprisingly, these methods have found particular application in monitoring environmental changes, improving the accuracy and depth of our understanding over more traditional methods.

It is important to note that machine learning is not a unitary concept. It encompasses multiple branches, each with different strengths and appropriate use cases. Supervised learning, unsupervised learning, reinforced learning, and deep learning all offer different vantage points in understanding environmental shifts. These methods leverage algorithms to sift through unmanageable volumes of data and filter out the meaningful signals that might otherwise be lost.

7.2. Machine Learning's Role in Air Quality Mapping

The degradation of our air quality poses a ubiquitous threat to public health, with long-term exposure leading to severe respiratory diseases, circulatory problems, and chronic health conditions. Existing methodologies to monitor air quality, such as satellite imagery and sensor-based data collection, can be cumbersome, expensive, and time-consuming.

Leveraging ML in this sphere has enabled scientists to map air quality on an unprecedented scale, both spatially and temporally. Training ML algorithms using vast datasets that might include meteorological parameters such as temperature, pressure, humidity, and wind speed and direction, along with region-specific variables like industry, population density, and vehicular emissions, can predict pollutant concentrations with remarkable precision.

Quick and inexpensive to implement, these tools can provide real-time air quality assessment, and offer significant advantages over tradition methods. They also allow for the identification of areas of particular concern, so that remedial efforts can be more effectively allocated.

7.3. Machine Learning and Monitoring Ocean Concerns

The oceans, covering more than 70% of the Earth, are pivotal regulators of climate conditions and harbors of biodiversity. They also present a vast data source that is still relatively untapped, owing to their navigating, exploring, and monitoring challenges. Marine studies, therefore, are overwhelmingly reliant on satellite data due to the logistical constraints of maintaining a global in situ sensor network.

Machine Learning is breaking new ground here, particularly with unsupervised techniques that can process large amounts of satellite data and reveal patterns and anomalies that can be indicative of phenomena like algal blooms, marine heatwaves, pollution spills, or shifting ocean currents. The implications of these change indicators range from biodiversity conservation concerns to the fishing industry's variations.

Chapter 8. Assessing Deforestation With Machine Learning

The rampant pace of deforestation has disturbing implications for biodiversity losses and greenhouse gas emissions. The traditional methods of quantifying deforestation, such as manual interpretation of satellite images, are time-consuming and often struggle to keep pace with the rapid progression of habitat loss.

Machine learning, however, can analyze imagery data over vast geographical scales at a refresh rate that is orders of magnitude more effective than human-led processes. By using supervised learning algorithms trained with historically validated deforestation imagery, these tools can detect fluctuations in forest cover, track the progression of deforestation, and even make projections about future deforestation pathways.

8.1. Conclusions

Climate change is the defining issue of our time, and machine learning is proving to be an effective instrument in documenting and understanding it. The advent of ML brings new avenues of promise to areas that desperately require detailed monitoring.

However, as we step further into leveraging machine learning in these applications, we need to be mindful of the limitations. Inconsistencies in data quality, the need for large and diversified training datasets, and problems tied with overfitting and poor transferability of models remain points of concern that warrant attention.

Overall, while machine learning is not a panacea for our

environmental concerns, it provides us with sharper tools for uncovering the full scope of our climate crisis. This understanding carries the potential to guide our mitigation efforts more effectively and foster a more sustainable coexistence relationship with our planet.

Chapter 9. Data Processing in Meteorology: The Machine Learning Strategy

Understanding data processing in meteorology in the context of machine learning strategies calls for appreciating the quantity, variety, and richness of data at hand. It also necessitates mapping how machine learning can extract maximum value from this data, transforming a sea of information into a wellspring of insights that help in predicting and understanding weather patterns and climatic changes.

9.1. The Essence of Meteorological Data

Meteorological data is an intricate tapestry of diverse measurements such as temperature, humidity, wind speed, precipitation level, and atmospheric pressure. They are logged from sources such as ground weather stations, weather balloons, radar systems, satellites, and even ships and aircraft. This staggering range and volume of data create an ideal environment for machine learning to operate, discern patterns and make detailed predictions.

9.2. Preprocessing: Transforming Raw Data

Like in all fields, in meteorology too, a careful preprocessing of raw data precedes the application of machine learning algorithms. This includes handling missing values, outlier detection and handling, data harmonization, and data transformation.

Missing values in meteorology datasets arise from instrument malfunction, system errors, or other unforeseen changes. These gaps are usually addressed through imputation strategies, kinematic interpolation, or more advanced techniques like multiple imputations or modelling.

Data harmonization blends together data collected from varied sources with different base standards, making it standardized and suitable for further steps in the machine learning pipeline. This process involves adjusting for differences in measuring instruments, techniques, and base conditions. It also includes steps like unit conversion and aligning disparate timescales.

9.3. Feature Engineering: Extracting The Vital

Feature engineering, a pivotal step, involves creating new variables – also known as features – that can help predictive models perform better. In meteorology, these may include indicators that combine multiple variables, temporal trends, patterns, or lagged variables. For instance, creating a feature that captures the rate of change of temperature between two consecutive time points offers valuable inputs into temperature prediction models.

9.4. Data Normalization: Leveling the Field

Data normalization is a critical process to rectify biases caused by the varying scales of different features in the dataset. By bringing the entire dataset to the same scale, more comfortable comparisons and more accurate predictions can be achieved. Two common techniques are min-max normalization and z-score standardization.

9.5. Dimensionality Reduction: Simplifying Complexity

Given the high-dimensional nature of meteorological data, it is essential to judiciously reduce the dimensionality of the dataset. Sparing computational resources and avoiding the 'curse of dimensionality,' techniques like Principal Component Analysis (PCA) and t-Distributed Stochastic Neighbor Embedding (t-SNE) help simplify high-dimensional data.

9.6. The Role of Time Series Data in Weather Forecasting

Time-series data forms the bedrock of meteorological studies due to the criticality of temporal trends in understanding weather patterns. Autoregressive Integrated Moving Average (ARIMA) models have long been used for weather forecasting. Recently, emerging techniques like Recurrent Neural Networks (RNNs) and Long Short-Term Memory (LSTM) Networks have dramatically improved the accuracy of these predictions.

9.7. Embracing Uncertainty: Probabilistic Forecasting

The inherent unpredictability in the atmosphere necessitates probabilistic forecasts. Machine learning models like Bayesian Neural Networks and Gaussian Processes embrace this uncertainty and provide ranges of forecasts rather than single point predictions.

9.8. Training and Validation: Ensuring Robust Models

Finalizing the machine learning model involves two crucial steps: training and validation. Training the model involves feeding it the processed data, optimizing model parameters to reduce prediction errors. Validation, on the other hand, is testing the model on unseen data to ensure its accuracy and robustness. Both steps go hand-in-hand and are iteratively performed to achieve the best model. Different techniques like k-fold cross-validation, stratified sampling, and time-series cross-validation are used to safeguard against overfitting and ensure model generalizability.

Data processing in meteorology using machine learning is not just about applying algorithms to data. It's a uniquely complex dance of technology and nature, where massive amounts of intricate data are cleaned, restructured, and transformed, paving the way for machines to learn from them, ultimately culminating in surprising insights about our atmosphere and predictions that promise to revolutionize weather forecasting and climate science. Not merely a dry academic exercise, it is a critical cog turning the wheel of our understanding of the earth's climate.

Chapter 10. Impact of Machine Learning on Climate Policy Decisions

Climate change, without a doubt, is the most pressing concern of the 21st century. For policymakers globally, finding a balance between economic development and environmental sustainability is a formidable challenge. With the advent of innovative technologies such as machine learning, handling these crucial decisions has become more manageable and accurate.

10.1. The Interface of Machine Learning and Climate Policy

Scientists have employed machine learning (ML) to develop an array of models to study temperature increases, precipitation changes, extreme weather events, and the subsequent influence on ecosystems and human societies.

These models not only quantify climate change but also suggest ways to address it. Policymakers can leverage these insights to forecast climate impacts better, formulate mitigation strategies, and adapt to changing circumstances. In essence, machine learning forms an indispensable bridge between climate science and policy decisions.

For example, ML algorithms can be trained to identify patterns in historical and current climate data, from which they can extrapolate future scenarios. In turn, these predicted scenarios inform climate policies and drive decision-making processes.

10.2. Machine Learning in Mitigation Strategies

The implementation of machine learning in mitigation policies has shown promising results. Techniques such as neural networks and decision trees have been applied to energy systems modeling, providing policymakers with reliable information to base emission reduction targets.

Precise ML models can forecast future energy demands and suggest the most efficient combination of resources to meet them, all while considering environmental impacts. ML algorithms can analyze patterns in energy consumption on a broader scale, pinpointing sectors where energy efficiency can be improved and emissions can be mitigated.

Similarly, ML can be utilized in the management of agricultural practices, an area often overlooked in emission reduction strategies. ML models can analyze data from different cropping systems, soil types, and climate conditions to suggest the most sustainable agricultural practices, thereby indirectly influencing climate policies.

10.3. Machine Learning in Climate Adaptation Planning

The capability of ML to analyze vast data sets and generate reliable predictions has made it an invaluable tool in climate adaptation planning. With intense weather events becoming the norm, there is an urgent need to build resilience in affected communities, and here, ML can offer remarkable assistance.

ML models can predict and quantify future climatic events and their potential impacts on social and infrastructural systems. These predictive models provide crucial inputs for establishing climate-resilient infrastructure and designing effective disaster management policies.

Moreover, ML's proficiency in pattern recognition can help in predicting climate-induced migration. Identifying the regions from where people are likely to migrate due to climate change can help in proactive planning and resource allocation.

10.4. Machine Learning in Climate Finance

Climate finance is another area where machine learning can have substantial impacts. ML can help in identifying the most effective strategies for climate change mitigation and adaptation investments, leading to better utilization of financial resources.

For example, ML models can assess the economic impacts of carbon pricing, enabling insightful decisions about policy design and revenue use. Furthermore, ML can also manage risks associated with climate investments, making the financial sector more resilient to the uncertainties of climate change.

10.5. Future Challenges and Prospects

While ML offers much promise in the world of climate policy decisions, it is not without its challenges. One key hurdle is the risk of algorithmic bias and the potential for inaccurate predictions. The quality of the ML models' results depends heavily on the quality of the data fed to them, meaning any inaccuracies or biases in the data could lead to flawed outputs.

Another challenge is the explanation of ML output. In many instances, even the designers of the ML models can find it hard to understand the underlying decision-making processes, leading to potential distrust.

Despite these challenges, the potential of machine learning for climate policy decisions is vast. With continued research and meticulous attention to data quality and interpretability, machine learning can become a cornerstone in the development of effective, sustainable climate policies.

As we venture deeper into the era of machine learning, it's clear that its role in climate policy decisions will only become more integral. Through refined predictions, improved efficiency, and effective resource allocation, ML holds the promise of a better, more sustainable future. By demystifying this technology, we can harness its power to fight climate change and shape resilient societies. Machine Learning is not only a tool for climate scientists; it's a companion for policymakers striving to leave behind a viable planet for future generations.

Chapter 11. Unlocking Weather Patterns and Complex Simulations

Weather prediction involves analyzing a wealth of historical meteorological data to understand past patterns and predict future ones. At its core, weather prediction is a complex data-analysis-driven mechanism that today, increasingly adopts the tools and techniques of machine learning to augment human expertise.

11.1. Leveraging Machine Learning in Weather Predictions

Machine learning, a branch of artificial intelligence, involves the training of algorithms to learn from data and make data-driven predictions or decisions. Given the extraordinary and increasing volume of data that meteorologists deal with, machine learning is a natural fit for the field. Weather patterns are essentially complex data patterns, and machine learning is specialized in recognizing and learning from such complex data.

Machine learning has the unique feature of delivering better performance as more data is fed into the system. This scalability is especially beneficial in weather prediction, as data is incessantly acquired from myriad sources such as satellites, radars, weather stations, and even mobile devices. Using deep neural networks, a type of machine learning, meteorologists can extract relevant information from this massive data set and make incredibly accurate forecasts.

11.2. Understanding Weather Data Complexity

Weather is impacted by numerous factors, each of which adds a different layer of complexity. Temperature, humidity, wind speed, and direction all interact to produce a range of weather phenomena, from a pleasant sunny day to a destructive hurricane. Recent developments in IT infrastructure enable this vast and varied stream of data to be collected and stored, a task which would have been inconceivably large-scale even a few decades ago.

But possessing a massive volume of raw data is only the first step - the true challenge lies in making sense of it. This is where machine learning shines. Machine learning can analyze complex datasets, identify hidden patterns, and distill this information into accurate weather forecasts.

11.3. The Role of Machine Learning in Climate Simulations

Beyond immediate weather predictions, machine learning is instrumental in contributing to climate simulations – complex computational models that try to replicate earth's climate and predict how it might change over the long term. Climate simulation models are crucial for preparing for and mitigating the impacts of climate change.

Machine learning helps refine these models, making them more accurate and reliable. Given the huge amount of variables involved – from solar radiation to industrial pollution – accurate climate simulation is an incredibly challenging task. However, machine learning can handle this complexity and bring forth insights that human analysis might overlook.

11.4. Case Study: Improved Forecasting through Machine Learning

To understand the practical application of machine learning in meteorology, consider the case study of the Meteorological Service Singapore (MSS). MSS uses a machine learning model that predicts rainfall in the next five minutes based on radar readings, with an accuracy rate of over 85%. The system uses machine learning to find patterns in past radar readings and predict future rainfall trends. The results have substantially improved the accuracy and timeliness of weather forecasts in Singapore, helping residents plan their activities more effectively.

11.5. Transforming Disaster Response

Machine learning is not only about predictions but can also inform response efforts during weather-related disasters. For instance, machine learning algorithms can predict the path of hurricanes and other calamities, giving disaster response agencies more time to prepare and act. In places susceptible to wildfires, machine learning models can predict the probability of fire occurrence and help authorities mitigate potential risks.

In conclusion, machine learning is carving out a significant role in meteorology and climate science. From deciphering weather patterns and enhancing climate simulation models to informing effective disaster response, machine learning brings new capabilities to these vital fields of study. As machine learning technology grows more sophisticated, its applications in understanding and predicting our weather and climate will only broaden, promising exciting developments in the future.

Chapter 12. Case Studies: Success Stories in Machine Learning and Meteorology

The first story of triumph in the junction of machine learning and meteorology comes from across the pond in the UK. Their esteemed Met Office, also known as the Meteorological Office, formerly a small operation modest in size but vast in ambition, has harnessed the potential of machine learning with incredible results.

12.1. The Met Office: Introducing Machine Learning to Forecasting

Until recently, the Met Office utilized traditional statistical models, namely general circulation models (GCMs) to forecast weather conditions. These models simulate the large-scale movements of air through different layers of the Earth's atmosphere and are effective in providing a generalized idea of weather patterns.

However, what was lacking was the ability to tackle the intricate smaller-scale meteorological phenomena with astute precision. The use of machine learning has changed this dramatically. In recent years, the Met Office has incorporated artificial intelligence into their forecasting arsenal, from optimizing the performance of their supercomputers to implementing machine learning algorithms for identifying patterns in weather situations quicker than a human could.

One such instance is the application of machine learning in generating highly accurate representations of the Earth's atmosphere. These numerical models called Neural Nets are applied to generate an optimized atmospheric model. Trained on an extensive dataset of past weather conditions, these Neural Nets are capable of identifying complex climate patterns with high precision.

12.2. Colorado State University: An Early Warning System for Severe Weather

On the other side of the Atlantic, researchers at Colorado State University have won accolades in using machine learning to develop an early warning system for severe weather conditions. Named the Dynamic Extended-Range Hydrologic Prediction System, the project successfully marries meteorology, hydrology, and machine learning.

The system takes into account various factors including snowmelt levels, soil moisture, and existing weather forecasts to predict water flows in rivers and streams up to one month in advance. In effect, this innovative system can forewarn about upcoming floods or drought conditions which demand immediate attention, thereby playing a pivotal role in disaster management.

As a testament to the power of machine learning, this early warning system moves beyond sensing weather conditions and instead acts as a predictive tool, demonstrating how machine learning algorithms can successfully forecast upcoming changes in weather patterns.

12.3. IBM's Deep Thunder: Accurate Predictive Models for Business

Exploiting machine learning technologies for weather prediction isn't only limited to meteorological offices or research universities. The private sector is also a notable player, with an outstanding example being IBM's Deep Thunder.

Launched as an ambitious project from IBM's Thomas J. Watson Research Center, Deep Thunder aimed at creating hyper-local weather forecasts, linking meteorology and machine learning to aid businesses in strategy and decision-making. Employing high-resolution, physics-based models and machine learning, Deep

Thunder provides customized short-term weather forecasts specific to a geographic location.

The distinguishing feature of Deep Thunder's model is its ability to translate meteorological data into business-specific insight. This can range from helping utility companies prepare for potential power outages, to aiding retail businesses in predicting consumer behavior patterns during particular weather conditions. With the power of Deep Thunder, businesses can prepare and strategize with the conditions of the sky as an ally, marking another successful union of machine learning and meteorology.

12.4. NOAA's HRRR Model: Hourly Updated Weather Predictions

Our exploration across success stories in the incorporation of machine learning in meteorology will be incomplete without including the achievements of the National Oceanic and Atmospheric Administration's (NOAA) High-Resolution Rapid Refresh (HRRR) model.

HRRR has used machine learning extensively for conducting hourly updated weather predictions that capture various atmospheric features ranging from heavy rainfall, wildfires, to aerosol concentrations. Machine learning has enabled NOAA to capture even the smallest discrepancies in temperature, wind speed, and other weather elements to present an exceptionally detailed real-time weather scenario. Therefore, HRRR is not only tremendously useful for weather forecasting but also instrumental in identifying potential weather disasters and aiding in disaster management.

These are just a fraction of the stratospheric leaps and bounds within the last decade in our ability to predict and react to the weather, guided by the hand of machine learning. Each one of these trailblazers has taught us that the integration of machine learning in traditional meteorology is not only a scientific novelty, but it is emerging as a world-changing force - one that brings us closer to understanding our natural world, protects our societies, and lifts our businesses to new heights. As our journey continues, it's safe to say that we're only at the dawn of this exploration, with more triumphs—and more success stories—still waiting just over the forecasted horizon.

www.ingramcontent.com/pod-product-compliance
Lightning Source LLC
Chambersburg PA
CBHW061055050326

40690CB00012B/2630